The Château of Chantilly

text
Nicole Garnier

photography
Pierre Bérenger and Giraudon

translation
Atlantique Traduction

2.

Cover:
View of the Château
of Chantilly

Vignette:
From left to right,

1.
The Book of Hours
of the Duke of Berry. April.
© Bridgeman-Giraudon

2.
Léon Bonnat.
Duke of Aumale, 1880.
© Bridgeman-Giraudon

History and architecture

The Middle Ages: From the Bouteillers to the Orgemonts

From the 10th to the 14th centuries, Chantilly belonged to the Le Bouteiller family, lords of Senlis. They had the first castle built, nothing of which now remains. In 1386, the heirs of Guillaume Le Bouteiller – who had been ruined by the *Jacquerie* (peasants' revolt) of 1358 – sold Chantilly to Pierre d'Orgemont, former chancellor to King Charles V.

Between 1386 and 1394, Pierre d'Orgemont had a medieval fortress, enclosed within seven pointed tours, built on a small rocky island set in the marshy Nonette valley. Nothing now remains of that castle except the tower foundations, which are washed by the moat and determine the triangular shape of the present-day *Grand Château.*

Not having a direct heir, Pierre d'Orgemont bequeathed Chantilly in 1484 to his nephew, Guillaume de Montmorency. In 1522, the latter gave up Ecouen, Montmorency and Chantilly to his son, the Constable Anne.

The Montmorencys at Chantilly (1484-1632)

The Constable Anne de Montmorency (1493-1567) is one of the greatest Renaissance figures. He was a comrade in arms of François I at Marignan, was taken prisoner at Pavia and was again in favour during the reigns of Henri II and Charles IX. He opposed the power of the Guise family and fought the Protestants relentlessly. In 1562, this rough soldier had his jaw smashed by a pistol shot at the battle of Dreux. He died in 1567, at the age of 74, at the battle of Saint-Denis. Two of his great-grandsons were, like him, great soldiers: Turenne and the Great Condé, who owned Chantilly in the 17th century.

This passion for war was combined in Anne de Montmorency with a pronounced liking for the arts. His campaigns in Italy had revealed Renaissance aesthetics to him so he had the medieval castle of the Orgemonts renovated by the architect Pierre Chambiges. Chambiges did not change the external appearance of the castle much but refurbished the frontages to the courtyard. Around 1560, Anne de Montmorency commissioned the architect Jean Bullant, whose work at Ecouen he had appreciated, to construct a second

1.

château, on an islet south of the castle. This was to be the *Capitainerie* or *Petit Château*, a rectangular building which has remained almost unchanged but was then separated from the *Grand Château* by a channel (filled in in the 19th century), which crossed what are now the courtyard of the *Capitainerie* and the aviary garden. A two-level walkway linked the two châteaux, and the *Capitainerie* could also be reached by a drawbridge which was removed in the 19th century and installed on the east wall, under the archway showing the Montmorencys' arms. The walls of the *Capitainerie* are reflected in the pool – a typical Renaissance touch – and are punctuated by dormer windows which break the entablature and stand out against the slate roofs. This is the oldest surviving part of the château.

Anne de Montmorency also had the terrace – where Paul Dubois's equestrian statue (1886) now stands – laid out and had seven chapels built on the estate. There remain two of these – the St Jean and St Paul Chapels – in the park and one – the St Croix Chapel – on the lawn facing the château.

1.
Lieven Cruyl.
The Château of Chantilly around 1680.
This view, painted just before the death of the Great Condé, shows the medieval fortress of the Orgemonts, built in the late 14th century, still standing in the middle of the French garden designed by Le Nôtre for the Great Condé.
© Bridgeman-Giraudon

2.

2.
The *Petit Château* or *Capitainerie* built around 1560 by architect Jean Bullant for the Constable Anne de Montmorency. To the south-east is the Jean-Bullant Lodge, a former entrance to the château, surmounted by the Constable's arms.

1.

Anne de Montmorency at Ecouen: collections at Chantilly

In around 1535, Anne de Montmorency had the Château of Ecouen (now housing the Musée national de la Renaissance) built, about 20 kilometres south of Chantilly. Part of the Ecouen collection was brought to Chantilly in the 19th century. Two enamelled earthenware panels representing scenes from Roman history can be seen in the main entrance lobby. They were made at Rouen by Masséot Abaquesne. In the chapel is the Ecouen altar, attributed to Jean Goujon, and two windows representing the Constable's sons and daughters. The passageways in the Tribune gallery have two carved reliefs; and 44 grisaille windows (1542-44), representing the love of Psyche and Cupid, were brought from Ecouen to Chantilly in the 19th century and now adorn the Psyche Gallery.

2.

The Constable's grandson, Henri II de Montmorency (1595-1632), built Sylvie's House in the park. He was beheaded at Toulouse in 1632 for revolting against King Louis XIII. Chantilly was then seized by Louis XIII, who often came here to hunt. He commissioned construction of the *Cabotière* building in the park, and his arms adorn the pediment.

The Condés at Chantilly (1643-1830)

In 1643, Anne of Austria (the wife of King Louis XIII) gave Chantilly to Charlotte-Marguerite de Montmorency, Princess of Condé and sister of Henri II de Montmorency, following the victory of her son, Louis II de Bourbon-Condé at Rocroi. The victor of Rocroi was called "The Great Condé" (1621-1686) and when he participated in the Fronde rebellion against King Louis XIV, Chantilly was seized. It was, however, returned to him after the Peace of the Pyrenees (1659). The Great Condé then transformed Chantilly, having the park designed by André Le Nôtre, who was later to work on the Versailles gardens. Le Nôtre channelled the Nonette, which crossed the estate

1.
Psyche windows, 1542-1544 from Ecouen). Psyche Gallery. Photo Giraudon.
The artefacts brought from Ecouen to Chantilly were masterpieces of the French Renaissance.

2.
Le Grand Degré, built for the Great Condé by Daniel Gittard and André Le Nôtre (17th century), dominates the French-style gardens.

3.
Le Grand Degré, statue by Jean Hardy (17th century).

The suicide of Vatel

In April 1671, the Great Condé received Louis XIV and all his court at Chantilly. His steward, Vatel, went down to the château's kitchens (now the Capitainerie restaurant) on the Friday morning – a day when no meat was eaten – and, finding a delivery of fish which was insufficient to feed the Court, fell on his sword. The other French ports were meanwhile delivering the fish on which so much depended. This incident, recounted in the letters of Madame de Sévigné, made the Great Condé's steward a model for French cooks.

from east to west, to create the *Grand Canal* (1671-73), and designed a branch, La Manche, the *Vertugadin* lawns and the French flowerbeds north of the château. He had Daniel Gittard build the monumental staircase called *Le Grand Degré* and designed the first maze. Le Nôtre moved the entrance to the château, creating the present view, and Mansart then built the two Pavilions of the main gate. To supply the fountains, the engineer de Manse built a lifting machine and dug enormous reservoirs in the lawn. The Orangery was completed in 1683.

The Great Condé made Chantilly a place of festivals, and there was a literary circle frequented by La Fontaine, La Bruyère, Bossuet, the Bishop of Meaux (who was to write the Great Condé's funeral oration), Madame de La Fayette and Madame de Sévigné. The two parallel walks flanking Le Nôtre's flowerbeds were called "philosophers' paths" in their honour. Molière put on a production of *Tartuffe* at Chantilly, and the Great Condé put on dances and firework displays in this enchanting location.

3.

The Great Condé's son, Prince Henry-Jules (1643-1709) had the *Grand Château* transformed by Jules Hardouin-Mansart, and the work was finished by Jean Aubert after Mansart's death. The walls and towers then took on the Classic layout which Chantilly was to have until the Revolution. An additional storey, with a balcony which went right round the château, enabled the numerous guests of the princes of Condé to be accommodated.

The Great Condé's great-grandson, Louis-Henri, known as Duke of Bourbon (1692-1740) was Louis XV's prime minister from 1723 to 1726. He had the Great Stables – an 18th century masterpiece – built by Jean Aubert. He decorated the apartments of the *Petit Château* magnificently, set up the Chantilly porcelain and painted canvas workshops, and had a natural history room arranged. To decorate the apartments, he called on Oudry, Desportes, Christophe Huet and Nattier.

When he died, his son, Louis-Joseph, Prince of Condé (1736-1818) was only four years old. On reaching adulthood, Louis-Joseph continued the embellishing, building the real tennis court (*Jeu de Paume*) in 1756 and the Château of Enghien between 1769 and 1772. The latter is the long classical building to the right of the main gate; it was constructed by Jean-François Leroy. Finally, in 1774, he had the Anglo-Chinese garden designed, and built the Hamlet, a group of seven country cottages (of which five survive) which was to inspire Queen Marie-Antoinette's hamlet at Trianon. He was widowed early and took part in the Seven Years' War, where he showed his military talent. Being hostile to the ideas of the Enlightenment and devoted to the monarchy. he emigrated with all his family after the fall of the Bastille. In 1792, he formed the émigré army, known as the army of Condé.

Chantilly during the Revolution

As the residence of the Bourbon-Condés who were cousins of the royal family, Chantilly suffered a great deal from the Revolution. The collections were seized and moved to the Central Museum of Arts (which was to become the Louvre), and the château became a prison. Starting in 1799, the buildings were handed over for demolition and all the upper floors of the *Grand Château* were destroyed. The orangery, theatre and

1.

1.
Hendrik-Frans De Cort. *The Château of Chantilly seen from the lawn*, 1781, shows the appearance of the château before the Revolution. To the left are the Great Stables (1719-35) and real tennis court (1756), which are still in existence. In the centre is the Orangery, which has been demolished. To the right is the *Grand Château* (demolished in 1799), with its high towers dominating Anne de Montmorency's *Petit Château* (16th century). The top storey of the *Grand Château* was used to house the numerous guests; it gave them a superb view over the gardens.

2.
J.-F. Leroy. *The Château of Enghien* (1769-72).

3.
Claudius Couton. *The Château of Chantilly*. Photograph taken in 1872, just before reconstruction of the *Grand Château* (1875-85).

menagerie were demolished, and part of the park was divided up and cleared. The real tennis court was only saved because of its conversion into a meeting room for patriots, and then into a café where people danced after the Revolutionary summer month of Thermidor.

The Restoration

After 1815, Prince Louis-Joseph returned from exile and tried to put the property in order. He had the ruined apartments restored and obtained the return of some of the pictures and *objets d'art* which had been seized during the revolution and remained in the *Louvre*. In 1817, he got the landscape architect Victor Dubois to design the English garden, between the château and the Great Stables. The ditch separating the two châteaux, which crossed the courtyard of the *Capitainerie* and the aviary garden, was then filled in.

His son, Louis-Henri-Joseph, Duke of Bourbon (1756-1830) had no direct heir as his son, the Duke of Enghien, had been shot in the Vincennes moat in 1804, on Bonaparte's orders. He therefore left his property to his great-nephew and godson, Henri d'Orléans, Duke of Aumale. The latter was the son of Louis-Philippe, Duke of Orléans, who became King of the French after the 1830 revolution.

3.

1.

Honoré Daumet and Reconstruction of the *Grand Château* (1875-85)

Under the July Monarchy (1830-48) the young Duke of Aumale got Eugène Lami to decorate his private apartments (1845) for himself and his wife. He had his architect, Duban, build the wooden gallery (1846) which bears his name and thought about having the *Grand Château* rebuilt. He had to leave France after the revolution of February 1848, however, and remained in exile from 1848 to 1870.

It was only when he returned to France that the Duke of Aumale entrusted Honoré Daumet (1826-1911) with the reconstruction of the *Grand Château* (1875-85). The programme was very eclectic, new architecture having to blend in with the 16th to 18th century parts; it had to incorporate works of art inherited or acquired by the prince, and make references to the Duke of Aumale's ancestors at Chantilly. Daumet rebuilt the *Grand Château* on the foundations of the medieval towers and integrated the Renaissance buildings. The Michelangelo Gallery – so called as it is decorated with copies of Michelangelo's *Slaves* (in the Louvre but formerly owned by the Constable Anne de Montmorency and adorning the wall at Ecouen) – reminds one of the porch at Anet. The chapel was inspired by Ecouen, and includes the windows, altar and part of the woodwork. The Psyche

1.
The *Grand Château* and the chapel seen from the Constable's terrace. When the *Grand Château* was rebuilt, Daumet took his inspiration from 16th century architecture.

2.

3.

4.

The "H.O." monogram

Everywhere – on the ceilings, windows and even door handles – can be seen the monogram "H.O.". These are the initials of the owner, Henri d'Orléans, Duke of Aumale.

Gallery takes the place of a gallery built by Chambiges and includes windows depicting the story of Psyche: masterpieces of civil Renaissance work when they were made in 1542-44 for the château of Ecouen. The main vestibule, hewn out of rock and decorated with magnificent iron bannisters made by Moreau, is of similar scale to the staircase at the *Palais-Royal*. It incorporates Rouen ceramic paving made in the 16th century by Masséot Abaquesne. The ceiling is decorated with a large patriotic composition, *L'Espérance* (Hope) painted by Maillart. The *Galerie des Cerfs* (Deer – or Stags' – Gallery) takes its name from a building created by Anne de Montmorency in the park but subsequently destroyed. The gallery celebrates hunting – the main occupation of the owners of Chantilly over the centuries – and was designed to show the *Maximilian's Hunts* tapestry. The caisson ceiling bears the coats of arms of the various families which have owned Chantilly. The Library (*Cabinet des Livres*), arranged at the junction of the two châteaux, also uses heraldry on its ceiling to acknowledge the Great Condé's comrades in arms. The Tribune gallery has a hexagonal shape reminiscent of the similar room in the Uffizi Gallery in Florence, where the Grand Duke of Medici hung his masterpieces. The ceiling is decorated with scenes depicting the places where the Duke of Aumale lived. This princely residence is modern and gas-lit, with Chapu caryatids on the main staircase. In the Deer Gallery are lighting brackets with torchères, the flames having the shape of a fleur-de-lys: the Orléans arms.

2.
The main staircase (19th century).

3. and 4.
The *Grand Château* seen from the English garden.

1.
Léon Bonnat. *The Duke of Aumale in 1890*. Musée Condé, Chantilly. Widowed and having lost his children, the Duke of Aumale devoted himself to rebuilding Chantilly, which he bequeathed to the *Institut de France* in 1886.

2.
Hippolyte Bellangé. *The Duke of Aumale taking the Smalah of Abd el-Kader*, 16 May 1843. Musée Condé, Chantilly. The Duke of Aumale began his brief military career (1840-48) in Algeria by covering himself in glory during the renowned taking of the Smalah.

1.

The Duke of Aumale

Henri d'Orléans, Duke of Aumale (1822-1897) was eight years old in 1830 when his great-uncle the Duke of Bourbon, last prince of Condé, left him the Chantilly estate. He was the fifth son of King Louis-Philippe and studied at the Lycée Henri-IV before joining the army in 1840 and fighting alongside his elder brother, the Duke of Orléans, in Algeria. He distinguished himself in May 1843 by taking the *Smalah* of Abd el-Kader, the itinerant capital of the Arab chief who had revolted against French rule in Algeria. This military feat made the 21-year-old prince a popular hero. In 1844 he married his cousin, Princess Marie-Caroline de Bourbon-Siciles, daughter of the Prince of Salerno. When the 1848 revolution broke out, the prince was Governor General of Algeria. He immediately left Algiers with his family for London, and it was during his 24 years' exile, living in *Orleans House*, Twickenham, that he assembled the collection that can now be seen

at Chantilly. He returned to France in 1871, entering the Académie Française in that year (and becoming a member of the *Académie des Beaux-arts* in 1880) and presiding over the trial of Marshal Bazaine. He had the *Grand Château* at Chantilly rebuilt by the architect Honoré Daumet as a showcase for his collections, and in 1884 bequeathed Chantilly to the *Institut de France* on condition that it be made a museum open to the public. Exiled again in 1886 and threatened with seizure of his property, he changed his will into an immediate donation, subject to a life tenancy. In 1889 he was elected to the *Académie des Sciences Morales et Politiques* and was recalled to France. He completed his work at Chantilly, acquiring further major works such as Corot's *Pastoral Concert* (in 1890) through art trading, and finishing hanging his collections in the château which he had chosen to make a museum.

2.

The Condé Museum: An Introduction to the 19th Century

The Chantilly château rebuilt by Daumet is a prince's residence but it is also, and even more, a museum and art gallery. The Duke of Aumale, who had lost his wife and two sons between 1866 and 1872, wanted from the beginning to make Chantilly a museum which would bear his family name Condé, which should have been carried on by the son who had died at the age of 21.

Honoré Daumet therefore designed several rooms right from the start as a museum, with its own entrance. [After the 1886 bequest, he added the Residence Wing, originally devoted to apartments for the prince's relations and guests, where very different choices were made.] The Picture Gallery (*Galerie de Peinture*), the main room of the Condé Museum, is an enormous space with rounded corners, lit by overhead windows. The works of art are shown frame-to-frame on Pompeiian red picture rails. Other rooms have walls covered in red velvet or are painted deep green, like the Tribune and Psyche galleries respectively. The pictures are arranged according to their dimensions, with no chronological or geographical logic. Only shapes and the whim of the curator guided the arrangement. The most that can be said is that in the Picture Gallery the left-hand wall displays pictures of or painted in Italy (by Poussin and Dughet), while the wall on the right shows those of the French school. Nineteenth century displays were characterised by dark tones, lighting from above, and mixing up of all periods and all schools. All collections of paintings, whether public or private, were then shown like that. The Duke of Aumale did, however, forbid two things in his will: the Condé Museum may neither lend its collections to any other institution nor change the way the works are displayed. Chantilly thus provides a fascinating testimony of what 19th century museums were like.

Before the 1848 revolution, the Duke of Aumale already had an impressive collection of paintings (by Van Dyck, Nattier and Oudry) inherited from the Condés. These were complemented by his first acquisitions, especially the 17th and 18th century historical portraits by Largillière, Drouais and

1.
The Orléans Room (Chantilly porcelain and lace). At the end are the Caroline and Clouet rooms.

2.
The Picture Gallery is typical of 19th century museum displays. The Duke of Aumale desired in his will that this arrangement be retained.
In the centre is a marble bust of the duke by Paul Dubois.

1.

Duplessis and the "oriental" works, which were much appreciated by the victor of Abd el-Kader. The Duke of Aumale bought back works which had come from the Orléans collection, dispersed in 1791, or from that of his father, King Louis-Philippe or his brother, Duke of Orléans. Examples are, respectively, Raphael's *Virgin of the House of Orléans*; J.-F. de Troy's Oyster *Lunch* and Nicolas Lancret's *Ham Lunch*; Delaroche's *Assassination of the Duke of Guise* and *Ingres's Malady of Antiochus.* He sometimes bought complete collections, like the drawings of Frédéric Reiset, Curator of the Louvre, the Italian paintings of his father-in-law, Prince of Salerno, and the portraits by Lenoir. He bought French masterpieces which he found abroad, in the hope of one day bringing them back to France. Examples are the *Book of Hours of the Duke of Berry*, the world's most beautiful manuscript, found at Genoa; three of his finest Poussins, including *The Massacre of the Innocents*; and the drawings of Carmontelle, found in England.

2.

A third Raphael identified at Chantilly in 1979

The Loreto Madonna, considered when in the Prince of Salerno's collection and then in the Duke of Aumale's as a copy of the lost original, was recognised as the original in 1979. Identification resulted from the inventory number it was given in the Borghese collection in Rome, and which can be seen low down on the left of the work.

1.

The richness and quality of its painting collection makes Chantilly the second-largest French art gallery, only exceeded by the Louvre. The Italian paintings include three of Raphael's masterpieces, among them the famous *Three Graces* (in the *Santuario*), inspired by a marble antiquity, and *The Loreto Madonna* (in the Rotunda of the Picture Gallery). There is a superb Sassetta, *The Marriage of St Francis to Poverty* (in the Tribune), which is part of a polyptych which was broken up. *The Portrait of Simonetta Vespucci* by Piero di Cosimo (in the Rotunda) shows the Grand Duke of Medici's mistress dead at the age of 23, with a perfect profile, the bust undraped and the serpent of immortality around her neck.

The French paintings are also highly representative of this school from the 15th to 19th centuries. The 15th century is illustrated by a superb retable by Enguerrand Quarton and Pierre Villate (in the Giotto Room), The *Virgin of Mercy*. This represents, according to a traditional iconography in the late Middle Ages, the Virgin covering with her robe the various categories in society, from the Pope, king and emperor to the clergy, laity and merchants.

The French Renaissance is represented by the Clouet Room, a whole room devoted to 16th century portraits. All the French monarchs of the period can be seen there: François I, Henri II, Charles IX, Henri III and Queen Catherine of Medici (four separate portraits). Other personalities portrayed are the writer Montaigne and the Constable Anne de Montmorency, builder of the *Petit Château* at Chantilly. This room combines part of the Duke of Aumale's collection and the Poncins-Biencourt donation of works by Montaigne to the Condé Museum, made in 1939.

French 17th century works include five original pictures by the great classical painter Nicolas Poussin (1594-1665), representing different periods of his artistic life. From his "Roman" youth are two mythological compositions – *Numa Pompilius* and *The Youth of Bacchus* (in the Picture Gallery) – and also a biblical scene of rare violence, *The Massacre of the Innocents*, painted for display over a door in a Roman

1.
Raphael.
The Loreto Madonna.

2.
Nicolas Poussin (1594-1665).
The Massacre of the Innocents is the finest work in the Condé Museum's collection of 17th century French paintings.

3.
The Clouet Room (with the Caroline Room at the end, on the left) displays French 16th century portraits. All the kings and queens of that period are represented.

2.

3.

palace but placed by the Duke of Aumale in the centre of the Picture Gallery with pride of place on the picture-rail. Unlike the artistic custom of his period, Poussin used a reduced range of colours and a small number of people to depict this tragic scene. This only serves to strengthen the horror of the scene: a mother in the foreground is screaming with grief and trying to stop a soldier who is going to kill her child. In contrast, Poussin's late style is represented by the *Landscape with Two Nymphs and a Snake* (in the Picture Gallery), where the importance given to people is reduced so as to leave room for meditation on nature. Pierre Mignard's superb *Portrait of Molière* (in the Tribune) completes the collection of 17th century paintings.

The French 18th century is represented by four paintings by Watteau. Together with *Love Disarmed* (in the Tribune) – a mythological scene, which is fairly surprising for this artist – the Condé Museum has three paintings which are more representative of Watteau, showing social mingling of the sexes: a genre which he

1.
Chantilly Château washed by the moat. On the left is the 19th century part rebuilt by H. Daumet for the Duke of Aumale.
In the centre is the *Capitainerie* (or Little Château), built in the 16th century by J. Bullant for the Constable Anne de Montmorency.
On the right is the Château of Enghien (18th century) with its classical lines, built by J.-F. Leroy.

2.
Piero di Cosimo
Portrait said to be of Simonetta Vespucci.

1.

2.

created. These are *Pastoral Pleasure* and two charming figures: *The Serenader* and *The Worried Lover* (in the Caroline Room). Facing them are four studies of heads by Jean-Baptiste Greuze, one of which – a *Head of Young Girl* – is apparently a sketch for *L'Accordée de village* (1761, in the Louvre). There are two masterpieces – J.-F. de Troy's Oyster Lunch and Nicolas Lancret's *Ham Lunch* (1735) – which were commissioned by King Louis XV for the dining room of the small apartments at Versailles and are typical of the 18th century *genre* in France. The first shows an aristocratic dinner with young lords eating oysters and drinking champagne – which had just been invented – while showing amusement at the cork popping out.

1.

1.
Ingres reworked his *Self-portrait at 24* a number of times and only finished it at the end of his life.

2.
Eugène Fromentin. *Heron-hunting in Algeria.* The Duke of Aumale collected a great many "orientalist" paintings, which reminded him of his youthful years spent in Algeria.

3.
Eugène Delacroix. *The Two Foscari.* Like all the other Romanticists, Delacroix was fond of colour. Here, he depicted a tragic story from Venetian history: the son of Doge Foscari, condemned for treason, beseeches his father.

4.
Jean-Antoine Watteau (1684-1721).
The Serenader is a work typical of this painter of mixed-sex gatherings.

2.

The 19th century is remarkably well represented at Chantilly. The Duke of Aumale collected works ranging from neo-classical to the end of the century but excluded the realists and the impressionists, of whom he was nevertheless a contemporary.

The neo-classical movement, which started early in the 19th century, was marked by the importance given to composition rather than colour, and a taste for antiquity. It is illustrated by Gérard's large picture *The Three Ages* (in the Picture Gallery, 1808 Room), the same painter's *Portrait of Bonaparte* (in the Tribune) and especially by Jean-Auguste Dominique Ingres's masterpieces (in the Tribune). Two of these are portraits (*Self-portrait at 24* and *Madame Devauçay*), and there is a large academic nude (*Venus Anadyomène*) and a historical painting (*Antiochus and Stratonice*).

The Romantic movement began in the 1830s and is represented by the work of Eugène Delacroix (*The Two Foscari* is in the Picture Gallery). This artist accompanied a French diplomatic mission to Morocco in 1832, discovered the light and colour of "the Orient" there and became leader of the "Orientalists" (*The Moroccan Guards* of 1847 is in the Isabelle Room). The Duke of Aumale, who had lived in Algeria from 1839 to 1848, was much attracted by "orientalism" and he therefore devoted part of the Picture Gallery (right-hand wall) to this artistic movement. The "orientalists" represented at Chantilly are, above all, Alexandre-Gabriel Decamps – of whom the Duke of Aumale was particularly fond, to the extent of placing the *Turkish Children at a Fountain* facing Poussin's *Massacre of the Innocents* – but also Horace Vernet, Marilhat, Ziem and Fromentin (whose *Heron-hunting in Algeria* is in the 1865 Room).

The Duke of Aumale, a former general, also acquired some military paintings by Meissonier (e.g. *Cavalrymen of 1805* in the Picture Gallery), Alphonse de Neville and Protais.

4.

3.

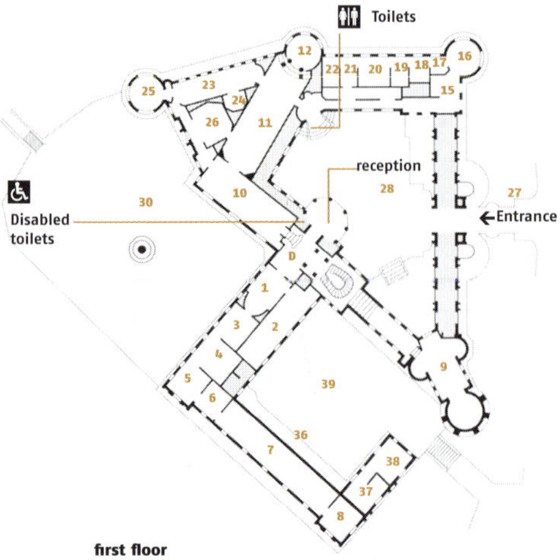

first floor
Same-level entrance from the Main Courtyard

THE GREAT APARTMENTS: Guided tours.
D. Assembly point from which guided tours start.
1. Antechamber: Hunting pictures by Oudry; mineralogical cabinet of the Princes of Condé, 1774.
2. Library: 13 000 books and 700 manuscripts.
3. Guards' Hall:
Portraits by Van Dyck; Herculaneum mosaic, *The Rape of Europe*.
4. Prince's Chamber: Riesener commode for Louis XVI's bedchamber at Versailles.
5. Grand Cabinet: 18th century woodwork.
6. Large Monkey Room: chinoiserie and monkey decorations by Christophe Huet, c. 1735.
7. Great Condé's Action Gallery: 11 large pictures of battles won by the Great Condé.
8. Music Room: 18th century furniture.
9. Chapel: Altar attributed to Jean Goujon; marquetry and 16th century stained-glass windows from Ecouen; Chapel of the Hearts of Condé with decoration sculpted by J. Sarrazin (17th century).

THE PICTURE GALLERIES: Open access.

10. Deer Gallery: Duke of Aumale's reception dining room (1880), decorated with hunting tapestries.
11. Picture Gallery: Paintings by Poussin, Champaigne, Nattier, de Troy, Fromentin, Delacroix, Gros and Corot.
12. Rotunda of the Picture Gallery: *The Loreto Madonna*, recognised as by Raphael in 1979; *Simonetta Vespucci* by Piero di Cosimo.
13 & 14. Logis Galleries: History of Chantilly Château.
15. Smalah Hall: Mementos from the Duke of Aumale's campaigns in Algeria and from Louis-Philippe and his family.
16. Minerva Rotunda: Portraits of the Orléans family (17th & 18th centuries); Tanagra statuettes.
17. Antiquities Room: Egyptian and Graeco-Roman statuettes; gold artefacts.
18. Giotto Room: 15th & 16th century Italian and French paintings (*The Virgin of Mercy* by Enguerrand Quarton).
19. Isabelle Room: 19th century paintings (by Delacroix, Boilly and Géricault).
20. Orléans Chamber: Chantilly porcelain (18th century) and Chantilly lace (19th century).
21. Caroline Room: 18th century French paintings (by Greuze and Watteau; Drouais's *Madame de Pompadour*).
22. Clouet Room: 90 16th century portraits of Renaissance kings and queens (François I, Henri II, Catherine of Medicis, etc.) by Clouet and Corneille de Lyon.
23. Psyche Gallery: 42 16th century stained-glass windows telling the story of Psyche and Cupid, made for the Constable de Montmorency.
24. Santuario: The *Three Graces* and the *Orléans Madonna* by Raphael; 40 illuminations by Jean Fouquet taken from the *Book of Hours of Etienne Chevalier.*
25. Jewel Room (Cabinet des Gemmes): Enamelwork and miniatures.
26. Tribune: Works by Sassetta, Poussin, Van Dyck, Champaigne, Mignard, Watteau, Delacroix, Ingres, etc.

37. Jean Bullant Room: Animal paintings by Christophe Huet (1735) and 18th century English fireplace.
38. Jean Bullant Bedchamber: English fireplace and alcoves from Twickenham (18th century).
37. and 38. can be visited with the private apartments (see page 22)
27. Entrance – 28. Main Courtyard
39. Capitainerie Courtyard
30. Aviary Garden

1.

The Great Apartments

Situated on the first floor of the *Petit Château*, in the wing dating from the Renaissance, the Great Apartments comprise three rooms decorated in 19th century style: the Library (*Cabinet des Livres*), the Guards' Hall and the Antechamber. This wing was built over the channel which used to separate the two châteaux. The Antechamber displays hunting pictures by Jean-Baptiste Oudry, commissioned for Chantilly in the 18th century, and also the mineralogical cabinet given to the Prince of Condé by King Gustave III of Sweden as a memento of his stay in Chantilly. This cabinet – together with some of the precious minerals which it contained but which were seized at the time of the Revolution – are now in the natural history room at the eastern end of the *Petit Château*. The Guards' Hall includes various military mementos under the portrait of the Great Condé and two portraits by the 17th century Flemish painter Van Dyck.

There is an apartment decorated with magnificent white woodwork and gold for the Duke of Bourbon, minister of Louis XV from 1723 to 1726. This comprises the Prince's Chamber and the Large Monkey

2.

3.

Room. The former no longer contains its original furniture, seized during the Revolution. It does, however, contain a commode commissioned from Reisener for King Louis XVI's bedchamber at Versailles and a corner cabinet with overdoor by Jean-Baptiste Le Paon representing *Sieges of the Great Condé*.
It became common in the 18th century to have whimsical decorations including monkeys or *chinoiserie*, together with rocaille motifs and white and gold wainscoting. Chantilly Château retains another room with such a decor inspired by the Far East, formerly attributed to Watteau but now acknowledged as the work of Christophe Huet. It was Huet who produced the monkey rooms in the château at Champs-sur-Marne and the Hôtel de Rohan in Paris, and also animal paintings in the Prince's Chamber at Chantilly.

The Large Monkey Room was painted in 1737. It is composed of painted panels and pier glass complemented by a completely decorated ceiling, and shows allegories of war, hunting, music, architecture and alchemy, the five senses and the four corners of the world. It forms part of the receiving apartments, and has a decorative appearance.

The sofa and chairs (late 18th century) come from Marie-Antoinette's bathroom at Versailles. Another chair has a back shaped like an anchor, indicating that it belonged to the Count of Toulouse, a great admiral of France; it came from the thatched cottage at Rambouillet. The fire screen showing a monkey as schoolmaster is also by Christophe Huet but is not originally from Chantilly; it was bought by the Duke of Aumale at a public sale in 1890 because its subject fitted in with the room's decor.

The Prince's Action Gallery is adorned with pictures showing the battles won by the Great Condé, who gave the painter, Sauveur Le Conte, all the necessary instructions but did not have the time to see them executed. At the back of the gallery, a filing cabinet which had belonged to La Live de Jully, who introduced ambassadors, dates from the mid-18th century and is one of the first neo-classical items of furniture. The tour finishes with the Music Room facing the late 18th century Château of Enghien which bears its name.

1.
The Prince's Chamber (early 18th century). (plan 4)

2.
The Large Monkey Room (1737). (plan 6)

3.
The Prince's Action Gallery, or Gallery of Battles (late 17th century). (plan 7)

2.

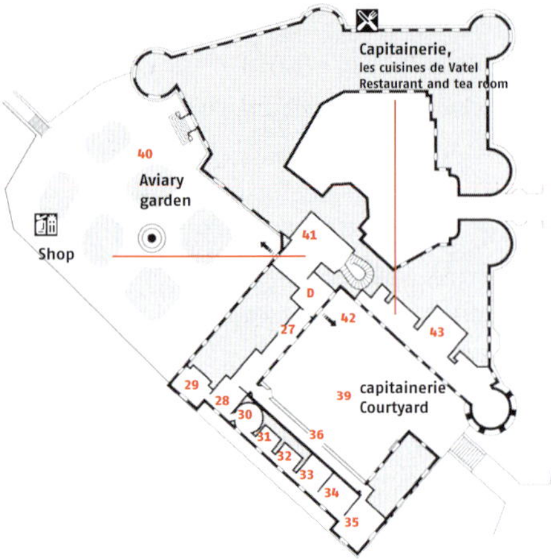

Ground floor
Reached by going down the main staircase or from the Capitainerie Courtyard and Aviary Garden level.
THE SMALL APARTMENTS: Guided tours in groups of 10 (tickets available from the shop).
These rooms were decorated (1845-6) by the painter Eugène Lami for the Duke of Aumale and the Duchess – Marie-Caroline de Bourbon-Siciles, Princess of Salerno – at the time of their marriage.
D. Assembly point from which guided tours start.
27. Daumet Gallery (1885-6): (Linking the *Grand Château* and the *Petit Château*): Woodwork, paintings and furniture.
28. De Guise Room (Duchess's Antechamber): Portraits of the Duke of Aumale and his sons.
29. Duchess of Aumale's bedroom: Bed with canopy, furniture with marquetry and portraits by Winterhalter of the duke and duchess at the time of their marriage.
30. Violet Room: Woodwork in rosewood and hangings of violet and silver brocaded satin; 18th century pastel drawings.
31. Small Monkey Room: Boudoir with monkey decorations painted by C. Huet in 1735 for the Duke of Bourbon.
32. Duke of Aumale's bathroom.
33. Duke of Aumale's bedroom: Above the camp bed is a portrait of the duke's mother, Queen Marie-Amélie, by Gérard.
34. Condé Room: 42 portraits of kings and queens of the House of Bourbon and princes and princesses of Bourbon-Condé.
35. Marble Room: Dining room and then library of the prince, in the Henri II style.
36. Duban Gallery (1846): Added to serve the Small Apartments, decorated with heraldic stained-glass windows (16th century) from Ecouen.
39. Capitainerie Courtyard
40. Aviary Garden – 41. Shop – 42. Exit
43. "La Capitainerie" Restaurant & Tea Room
First floor (see previous page)

The Private Apartments of the Duke and Duchess of Aumale

The private apartments of the Duke and Duchess of Aumale occupy the ground floor of the *Petit Château*. They include two galleries decorated with glazed woodwork and named after the architects who built them. The Daumet Gallery (1885-6), linking the *Grand Château* with the *Petit Château* is adorned with paintings by the German Joseph Rebell showing various locations in the Bay of Naples. The Duban Gallery (1846) was built, without structural work, on the courtyard of the *Capitainerie* to serve the Apartments, all the rooms of which interconnected. It incorporates the windows from Ecouen with the Montmorencys' coats of arms, and arms won in battle. Apart from the Small Monkey Room, an 18th century boudoir separating the duke's apartment from that of the duchess, the decor is 19th century. The Duke of Aumale entrusted the decoration to the painter Eugène Lami at the time of his marriage to his cousin Marie-

Caroline of Salerno (1844). This comfortable apartment with small rooms built over the moat looks onto the enormous balcony of the *Petit Château*. The Duchess did not live there long as she died in exile in 1869. It remains completely furnished in an eclectic style and is a perfect example of interior decorating under the July Monarchy.

The Guise Room, or Duchess's Antechamber, contains Robert-Fleury's *Portrait of the Duke of Aumale at the age of nine*, painted a year after the duke's great-uncle had left him Chantilly. There are also portraits of his two sons: *The Prince of Condé* (who died in 1866, at the age of 21) and *The Duke of Guise* (who died in 1872, aged 18), painted by Jalabert. The overdoors, painted by 19th century artists, depict various locations on the Chantilly estate at various times: *The Château at the time of the Great Condé* by C. Godefroy, *The Hamlet* by Français and *The Pack leaving the Great Stables* by Jean-Maxime Claude. The consoles carry a marble bust of the Duke of Aumale by Vilain and a Menessier bronze of the prince in the uniform of a general in the African army.

The Duchess's Bedroom (restored in 1971) contains a bed with a canopy and padded armchairs of Louis XV style. The ceiling was painted by N. Diaz in 1845 and shows birds balancing on a rose garland surrounding the duchess's initials (C.A.). The neo-gothic prayer stool is close to the wardrobe with marquetry by Grohé, decorated with plates of Sèvres porcelain. On either side of the chimney breast are portraits according to Winterhalter of the duke and duchess at the time of their marriage.

The Duchess's Boudoir, or Violet Room, was decorated by E. Lami in 1845-6 and is covered in violet satin brocaded with silver, which can also be seen on the screen and furnishings (reversed). The inlaid items of furniture, like the piano – which has a curved shape to fit in with the shape of the room – were made for the Duchess of Aumale by the Grohé brothers, cabinet makers to King Louis-Philippe. Pastel drawings from the 18th century show princes and princesses of the houses of Bourbon and Condé; one example is the Duke of Enghien, shown as a child to the left of the door, who was born in this room in 1772. The Duchess's Apartment therefore mixes examples of the Louis XV and Louis XVI styles.

3.

1.
The Duchess of Aumale's bedroom was decorated under the direction of Eugène Lami in 1845-6.
Photo P. Bérenger. (plan 29)

2.
The Violet Room, Duchess of Aumale's boudoir (1845-6). (plan 30)

3.
The Daumet Gallery (late 19th century) leads to the private apartments of the Duke and Duchess of Aumale. (plan 27)

The Small Monkey Room is the only remaining room in the Apartments of the Duke and Duchess of Aumale decorated in 18th century style. This very small boudoir is entirely covered with beautiful decorative panels illustrating in satirical manner the aristocratic entertainments of male and female monkeys during the various seasons, whose characteristics are shown in the lower panels. They pick cherries in spring, bathe in the summer, hunt – in the Chantilly forest, wearing the hunting costume of the House of Condé – in autumn, and skate on a frozen moat suggesting that of Chantilly in winter. The ceiling carries medallions of the seasons in monochrome blue, illustrating various of La Fontaine's Fables including *The Fox and the Stork, The Two Pigeons and The Fox and the Bust.*

The Duke of Aumale's Apartment is more austere, and was redecorated after his return from exile. It is reached via the bathroom, which is provided with hot and cold water; the small rooms had central heating and were lit by gas from 1886.

The Duke of Aumale's bedroom is embellished with superb early 18th century woodwork and was decorated in the mid-19th century with Romantic paintings by Eugène Lami, Camille Roqueplan and Baron, depicting life at Chantilly in the 16th, 17th and 18th centuries. Grohé's large roll-top desk (1845) was given by King Louis-Philippe to his son. Above the camp bed – of altogether military austerity – the Duke of Aumale kept Gérard's portrait of his mother, Marie-Amélie, Duchess of Orléans, around 1819-1820. There is a display cabinet containing the death mask of the Duke of Aumale, who died in Sicily in 1897.

The Condé Room (*Salon de Condé* or *Salon du Duc*), in the Louis XIV style, is covered with brocaded red silk damask and adorned with a monumental chimney breast of Renaissance inspiration and including a bust of the Duke of Bourbon (1756-1830). A series of 42 medallions by J.-M. Ribou (late 18th century)

1.

1.
Overview of the Small Monkey Room panels.
The Small Monkey Room (1735) was probably painted, like the Large Monkey Room, by Christophe Huet.
(plan 31)

2.
The Condé Room.
(plan 34)

2.

presents portraits of the kings and queens of the House of Bourbon and princes and princesses of the House of Bourbon-Condé. On the walls are family portraits including Ary Scheffer's *Queen Marie-Amélie*, Juste d'Egmont's *The Great Condé* (1621-1686) and Pierre Gobert's *Louis-Henri de Bourbon, Prince of Condé* (1692-1740).

The Marble Room is a Renaissance-style dining room with marble paving, a caisson ceiling, a chimney breast decorated with ancient coats of arms and 16th century furniture. Numerous mementos serve as reminders of the last owners of Chantilly.

1.

2.

3.

1.
Jar with lid, early 18th century.

2.
Duster, early 18th century. When it began, Chantilly porcelain copied Far Eastern motifs.

Chantilly Porcelain

In 1725, Louis-Henri de Bourbon started the manufacture of porcelain in the château basement. It was a soft porcelain made without kaolin (the first French deposits of which were only found in 1766, at Saint-Yrieix near Limoges).

This first factory made items with motifs inspired by the porcelain of the Far East, particularly the Kakiemon style (Chinese decoration using herons). Styles developed very quickly and around 1760 a very sober blue decoration on a white background gained ground against decoration with twigs or carnations. The factory mark, which was always put on the back of the items, was a hunting horn, serving as a reminder that Chantilly was above all a hunting residence for the Condés. The factory's output was small and it soon disappeared.

3.
The Book of Hours of the Duke of Berry. April.

The Library

The *Cabinet des Livres* is the largest library in France apart from the *Bibliothèque Nationale*. Among other things it holds 700 manuscripts, 300 of them illuminated, and 30 000 printed works including a beautiful collection of incunabula (books printed in the late 15th century, just after the invention of printing). The Duke of Aumale was a passionate bibliophile and himself drew up the catalogue (and there is a picture in this room showing him at work). Among his most beautiful acquisitions is the famous manuscript *The Book of Hours of the Duke of Berry*, illuminated by the Limbourg brothers for the brother of King Charles V and decorated with a calendar showing the twelve months; it was completed after the death of the Limbourg brothers, probably by Jean Colombe. The Duke of Aumale acquired it in 1856, when he was only 34. The other star items in this unique collection are the *Ingeburge Psalter* and the *breviary of Jeanne d'Evreux*. Display cabinets show manuscripts and printed and bound books and their contents are changed regularly.

Fouquet's 40 Miniatures

Forty miniatures by Jean Fouquet for the Book of Hours of Etienne Chevalier, Treasurer to King Charles VII, are exhibited in the Santuario of the Picture Gallery. Jean Fouquet was one of the first artists to introduce perspective in France, after his journey to Italy. This collection was removed from the *Book of Hours* (book of prayers for various times of day) in the 18th century

4.

5.

4.
Jean Fouquet. *Etienne Chevalier kneeling before the Virgin and Child.*

5.
The Ingeburge Psalter.

1.

The Great Stables

Between 1719 and 1735, the architect Jean Aubert built the monumental Great Stables of Chantilly, a masterpiece of 18th century French architecture, for Louis-Henri, Duke of Bourbon (1692-1740). It is said that the duke believed in metempsychosis and thought he would be reincarnated as a horse after his death. Contrary to the custom of the time, the building was erected at a distance from the château. It was 186 metres long and could accommodate 240 horses and 500 dogs. Above the ground floor is an Italian-style balustrade hiding the attic, and the central pavilion houses a fountain and drinking trough. Crowning this section is a statue of Fame, a recent replacement for Coysevox's original, which was melted down during the Revolution. The stalls are aligned along one of two enormous aisles. The building also houses a circular manege, kennels and storerooms. The sculpted decoration, produced under the direction of Rémy-François Bridault, depicts horses and hunting. When the prince died, in 1740, the building was still unfinished. The north-east wall, which was then being constructed and which straddled the road leading to the town of Chantilly, became the Saint-Denis gate.

In the 18th century, the Great Stables were used for festivities. All Chantilly's important guests visited them: Louis XV in 1769, the dauphine and the daughters of Louis XV in 1770, the King of Sweden in 1771, Emperor Joseph II, brother of Marie-Antoinette, in 1777 and Grand Duke Paul (later Tsar Paul I) in 1782. The birth of the Duke of Bourbon was celebrated on the 20th April 1756 with a great supper under the dome. In 1777, Princess Louise de Condé's departure from a convent was also celebrated there.

The Living Horse Museum

Since 1982, the Great Stables have housed the Living Horse Museum. The museum was created by Yves Bienaimé and, since it started, has shown horses of different breeds in their stalls. The public can see them undertaking their daily work, and there are educational equestrian demonstrations in the central rotunda three times a day. Horse shows are put on at certain times of year.

The Park

1.
The Great Stables' manege (1719–35) seen from the Real Tennis Court (1756).

2.
Aerial view of Chantilly Château, with the French gardens and racecourse on the left.

Le Nôtre's French Garden

André Le Nôtre designed a French-style park for the Great Condé before 1663 and worked with his nephew, the landscape architect Claude Desgots. From an area of marsh, Chantilly was to be transformed by Le Nôtre's work into an enchanting location which the numerous guests of the princes of Condé hastened to visit at festival times. There were frequent firework displays, concerts and dances.

Le Nôtre had to tame the watercourses. The Nonette was channelled and became the *Grand Canal,* crossing the park from east to west, and two great axes progressively became established, one parallel to *the Grand Canal* and the other at right angles to it. The latter starts at the main gate, climbs the Constable's Terrace and then goes down again along the *Grand Degré* towards the French flowerbeds (parterres) and the branch of the *Grand Canal* called *La Manche.* The view then continues upwards to the *Vertugadin,* an enormous semicircle of lawn facing the château, before losing itself in the forest.

2.

1.

It could be said that Chantilly was a draft for Versailles because Le Nôtre tested out his abilities in the former location before receiving Louis XIV's commission for the latter. Chantilly is, however, the only one of Le Nôtre's gardens where the château is not at the crossing point of the two main axes. Here, the château is actually to the side, and it is, instead, the equestrian statue of the Constable Anne de Montmorency which is at the focal point.

The Small Park

Early in the 18th century, the Duke of Bourbon used the wooded and higher part of the park to the south-east of the château and parterres for all sorts of entertainments. The most remarkable was a gigantic board (extant) for a game akin to snakes and ladders, where the pieces were the guests at the Chantilly parties. Commoner attractions in princely parks and to be found here were the games of real tennis and battoir, and of course a maze.

The Anglo-Chinese garden in the Hamlet

In the late 18th century there was a fashion, started by Jean-Jacques Rousseau and other philosophers, for nature and its charms. The Prince of Condé had his architect, Jean-François Leroy, build a group of cottages known as the Hamlet (1774), which served as the model for Queen Marie-Antoinette's Hamlet at Versailles. The cottages looked very rustic from the outside but were very luxuriously furnished inside; they were a place for the Condé family to relax and receive guests. In accordance with tastes at the time, there was an Anglo-Chinese garden surrounding the Hamlet. A network of small canals, crossed by rock bridges,

4.

2.

brought water to the area and facilitated pleasant boat trips from the Port des Pirogues (literally "dugout canoe port").

The English Garden (1817)

When he returned from exile, the Prince of Condé found the part of Le Nôtre's garden to the west of the château as far as the Great Stables, and from the Real Tennis Court to the Grand Canal, ruined. He commissioned the landscape architect Victor Dubois to design an English park in the Romantic style of the day. The English garden is all curves and distinguished by the absence of straight-line views; there is an irregular arrangement of plants, as if nature alone had influenced their location. A number of buildings, like the Temple of Venus, were put up in the English Garden, and the only trace of Le Nôtre's earlier splendour was the Beauvais Cascades, near the Real Tennis Court. The Pont des Grands-Hommes (Great Men's Bridge) now marks the boundary of the park which, before the Revolution, used to extend much further west, beyond the present-day town of Chantilly.

3.

5.

1.
The Hamlet 1774.

2.
Chantilly, Island of Love, in the English Garden.

3.
Le Nôtre's French gardens (parterres) with the part of the château rebuilt in the 19th century in the background. In the right background is the English garden (1817).

4.
The Real Tennis Court (1756–1758).

5.
The Beauvais Cascades, designed by André Le Nôtre (17th century).

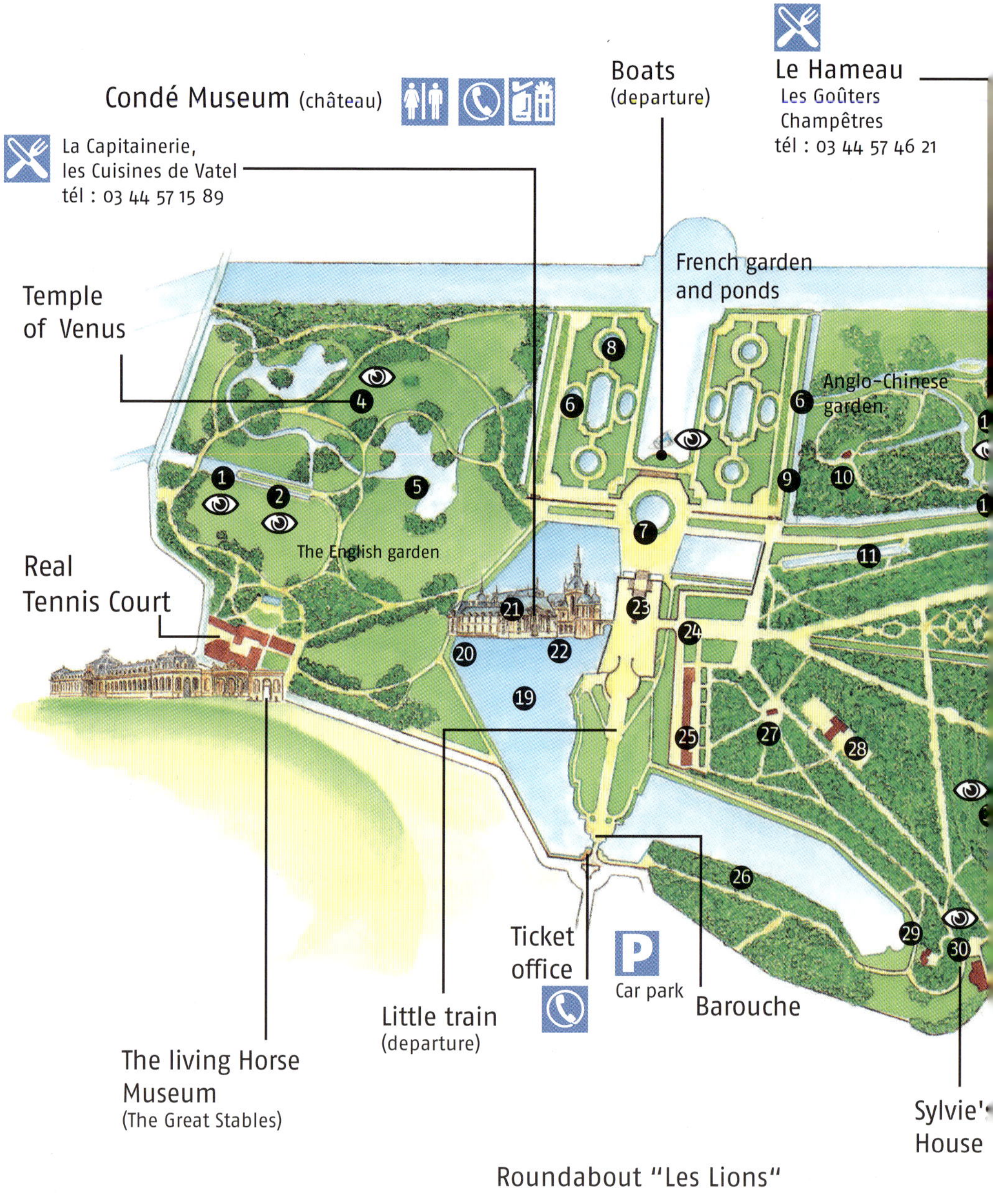
Condé Museum (château)
La Capitainerie,
les Cuisines de Vatel
tél : 03 44 57 15 89
Boats
(departure)
Le Hameau
Les Goûters
Champêtres
tél : 03 44 57 46 21
Temple
of Venus
French garden
and ponds
Anglo-Chinese
garden
The English garden
Real
Tennis Court
Ticket
office
Car park
Barouche
Little train
(departure)
The living Horse
Museum
(The Great Stables)
Sylvie's
House
Roundabout "Les Lions"
1
2
4
5
6
7
8
9
10
11
19
20
21
22
23
24
25
26
27
28
29
30

Chantilly racecourse
200 metres away
on the way to Paris,
La Table des Lions

Un personnage de Thierry Courtin

25, avenue Pierre-de-Coubertin, 75013 Paris
ISBN : 978-2-09-257438-6
Loi n°49-956 du 16 juillet 1949
sur les publications destinées à la jeunesse,
modifiée par la loi n°2011-525 du 17 mai 2011.

Achevé d'imprimer en janvier 2019 par Lego, Vicence, Italie.
N° d'éditeur : 10250719 - Dépôt légal : avril 2017.

T'choupi

va à la ferme

Illustrations de Thierry Courtin

T'choupi regarde les vaches
avec mamie.
– J'aimerais bien voir d'autres
animaux. On peut aller
à la ferme ?
– Très bonne idée, T'choupi :
Allons-y !

Voilà justement le fermier
sur son tracteur !
– Je peux monter dedans ?
demande T'choupi.

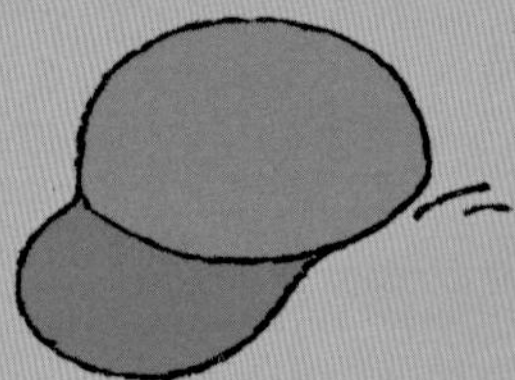

Le fermier sourit :
– Allez hop, en route :
direction la ferme.
– Youpi ! s'écrie T'choupi.
Tu as vu, mamie, c'est moi
qui conduis. Vroum-Vroum !

Le tracteur arrive à la ferme.
– Regarde mamie, il y a plein de petits poussins !
– Va voir dans le poulailler, T'choupi. Je suis sûre que les poules ont pondu des œufs ce matin.

– Oh là là, vous avez bien caché vos œufs, petites coquines… il m’en faut trois : un œuf pour ma mamie, un œuf pour mon papi et un très gros pour moi !

Quand T'choupi a fini,
il va voir les cochons.
– Ils sont rigolos, dit T'choupi.
Mais ils ne sentent pas très bon !

– Maintenant, allons voir
le petit agneau qui est né !
dit le fermier.
– Coucou brebis, dit T'choupi.
Il paraît que tu as un nouveau
bébé !

– Et voici le petit agneau !
Il n'a pas encore de prénom :
tu as une idée, T'choupi ?
– Hum… comme il est tout frisé,
on pourrait l'appeler… Frisouille !
– Quelle bonne idée ! Tu veux lui
donner son biberon ?

– Hi-hi-hi, Frisouille me fait des chatouilles ! Quel glouton, ce petit mouton.

– Bye-bye Frisouille,
mon copain tout frisé !
Je reviendrai bientôt
te voir avec ma mamie
et mon papi aussi.

Découvre d'autres aventures de T'choupi

1. veut un chaton
2. ne veut pas prêter
3. n'a plus sommeil
4. jardine
5. fait du vélo
6. est trop gourmand
7. est en colère
8. s'amuse sous la pluie
9. se déguise
10. fête Noël
11. se baigne
12. fait un bonhomme de neige
13. fait une cabane
14. rentre à l'école
15. a peur de l'orage
16. a une petite sœur
17. se perd au supermarché
18. prend le train
19. part en pique-nique
20. est malade
21. fait une surprise à maman
22. fête son anniversaire
23. a perdu Doudou
24. fête Halloween
25. fait un gâteau
26. va au cirque
27. fait de la musique
28. veut regarder la télé
29. fait un tour de manège
30. s'occupe bien de sa petite sœur
31. fait la sieste
32. est fâché contre papa
33. va sur le pot
34. a peur des chiens
35. cherche les œufs de Pâques
36. prend son bain
37. veut tout faire tout seul
38. aime la galette
39. ne veut pas se coucher
40. va à la piscine
41. fait des bêtises
42. part en vacances
43. est poli
44. s'habille tout seul
45. fait du poney
46. a une nouvelle nounou
47. a la varicelle
48. dort chez papi et mamie
49. bientôt grand frère
50. déménage
51. fait du bateau
52. mange à la cantine
53. a un bobo
54. a une amoureuse
55. va à la ferme
56. n'aime pas la bagarre
57. fait du ski
58. n'a plus de tétine
59. joue au tennis
60. dit non !